The Nature Walk

by Amy Leggett-Caldera
Illustrated by Gwen Keraval

PEARSON

Glenview, Illinois • Boston, Massachusetts
Chandler • Upper Saddle River, New Jersey

It is the first day of fall.
"Can we go for a walk?" Tina
asks Mother.
"Yes. We can go to the park,"
says Mother.

Tina, Mother, and Father
use their eyes to see things
in the park.

"Look! I see three blue eggs in a
bird's nest," says Tina.

Tina uses her nose to smell things.
She can smell the pine trees.
"These smell good," says Tina.

Tina uses her fingers to feel things.
She picks up a rock.
   "This rock feels smooth," says Tina.

"Listen, Tina. Can you hear the crickets?" asks Father. Tina tries to hear.

"I can hear them with my ears," says Tina.

Chirp, chirp, chirp.

see

smell

hear

feel

Tina uses her eyes to see things. What does she use to smell things?

Tina uses her ears to hear sounds. What does she use to feel things?

There are many ways to explore nature. What does Tina see in the park? What does she hear?